Acts of the Holy Spirit

Dr. Warren Lathem

Devotional Book
Acts of the Holy Spirit
by Dr. Warren Lathem

Design and Layout by Arnold Herrera

RJR Publishing
Lathemtown

ISBN
978-1-4357-6649-5
Lulu.com

Introduction
The Acts of the Holy Spirit

This is a devotional guide to the reading of the Book of Acts. You will read one chapter a day in Acts of the Apostles. Then you will read a short devotion based on that chapter. We trust you will be empowered to be witnesses as were the early Apostles.

Why did I entitle the book, "Acts of the Holy Spirit?" Many years ago, the great Professor of Evangelism, Robert Coleman, taught a course at Asbury Theological Seminary entitled, "Evangelism in the Book of Acts." It was an inductive study of Acts with a primary focus on Evangelism. I was privileged to be a student in his class in 1975.

Dr. Coleman postulated that since the Biblical Books did not originally contain titles, (those were assigned by later editors) the "Acts of the Apostles" title was non-canonical. He suggested a better title would be "The Acts of the Holy Spirit." His rationale was the primary narrative was the story of the work of the Holy Spirit in the lives and ministries of the Apostles. He further stated the ministry of the church today is often so anemic because of the lack of the power of the Holy Spirit working in and through the church.

It has been my privilege to use the material generated in Dr. Coleman's seminary class in an inductive Bible study in almost every church I have served as well as in some other churches. Further, it has been my privilege to teach this material in the Seminary in Venezuela. We founded this institution in 2002 and have watched the tremendous impact the Seminary has had on the life and growth of the church. The "signs and wonders" recorded in Acts are being repeated in Venezuela. This will be the case in any church empowered by the Holy Spirit.

For the second time, the Bishop in Venezuela is sharing these devotions with his pastors. He deems these reflections on Acts to be essential for pastors to understand the nature of effective ministry.

It is my prayer that the reader will have a deep and profound experience of the filling of the Holy Spirit and will see the results in your life and ministry. Since the Book of Acts has no conclusion, the Acts of the Holy Spirit continue through you!

Dedication

The Acts of the Holy Spirit is dedicated to the glory of God and in honor of Jared and Lim Lathem. They are currently planting a church in Cobb County, Georgia. They are the parents of our four grandchildren, Zoe, Elijah, Alana, and Zyana. Both Jared and Lim have faced some tough challenges in their individual lives and in their marriage. However, they have emerged victorious in the power of the Holy Spirit. Further, Jared preaches with a clear anointing of the Holy Spirit on his life and ministry. Lim is currently being admitted to Asbury Theological Seminary where she will pursue her call to a ministry in counseling. Jane and I could not be prouder of their lives and ministries. We declare power and freedom for them in the Holy Spirit.

Special Thanks

Thank you to Nisser and Arnold Herrera for their cover design, layout, and publishing on Lulu. We are grateful for this young couple who partner in ministry with us through their printing business in Venezuela making Spanish version resources available to the Seminario Wesleyano de Venezuela, the church in Venezuela, and to Spanish speakers around the world.

Thank you to Melissa Nobile, friend on FaceBook, and Blog writer friend of Jane. She edited this book, corrected my many mistakes, and made it appear to English teachers as if I remember all the grammar rules of my youth. I am especially indebted to her.

Instructions

In order to get the most out of these 28 days in Acts of the Apostles, I suggest the following:

1. ***Read the entire Book of Acts in one sitting.***
2. ***Read the Book of Acts a second time, reading it out loud so you can hear the flow of the narrative.***
3. ***Before reading the assigned chapter ask the Lord to speak to you in the reading.***
4. ***Each day read the assigned chapter before reading the devotion.***
5. ***Read the devotion.***
6. ***Pray. Ask the Holy to convict, convince, and purify your heart and life. Ask Him to pour his power into your life. Ask Him what you need to do in response to the revelation of the scripture reading for the day.***
7. ***Record your thoughts each day. Add to your prayer list.***

CONTENTS

Acts

Read Acts 1

Power

"Do not leave Jerusalem, but wait for the gift my Father promised, which you have heard me speak about. For John baptized with water, but in a few days you will be baptized with the Holy Spirit." "But you will receive power when the Holy Spirit comes on you; and you will be my witnesses in Jerusalem, and in all Judea and Samaria, and to the ends of the earth."

Acts 1:4b, 5, 8.

It is clear Jesus intended his followers to be baptized in the Holy Spirit. That same Holy Spirit baptism would give them the power necessary for effective ministry. This ministry of "being my witnesses" would propel them and subsequent spirit-baptized followers to the "ends of the earth."

Luke, the author of The Acts of the Apostles, would use verse 8 as the outline of this book showing how the spirit-baptized followers of Jesus would witness in "all Judea and Samaria, and to the ends of the earth." The last chapter, 28, seems to be missing an ending or conclusion. Some scholars think the last chapter or chapters were lost from

Power

the early manuscripts. However, most believe Luke ended his account of the Acts of the Apostles the way he did because the story was not yet finished. The work, the ministry, of spirit-baptized followers of Jesus would continue as they were witnesses of a Jesus to "the ends of the earth."

Have you been baptized in the Holy Spirit? Followers of the theology of John Wesley believe this is most often a "second work of grace." First, we are born again by the Spirit. Then, we realize we lack the kind of power necessary for holy living and effective ministry. We seek the fullness of the Holy Spirit - the baptism of the Holy Spirit. While new birth and baptism with the Holy Spirit may occur simultaneously for some, that is not the experience of most of us.

Do you have power for effective ministry? Do you have power for Holy living, for a consistent, obedient Christian life? Do you have power to have faith to be a witness of Jesus "to the ends of the earth? If so, praise the Lord! However, if not, today begin to pray and seek to be baptized in the Holy Spirit; to be filled by the Holy Spirit. The Lord is faithful. He will give you "the promise of the Father."

Thoughts of the day

Prayer list.

1.
2.
3.
4.
5.
6.
7.
8.

Read Acts 2

"Therefore let all Israel be assured of this: God has made this Jesus, whom you crucified, both Lord and Messiah." When the people heard this, they were cut to the heart and said to Peter and the other apostles, "Brothers, what shall we do?" Peter replied, "Repent and be baptized, every one of you, in the name of Jesus Christ for the forgiveness of your sins. And you will receive the gift of the Holy Spirit.

Acts 2:37-39

This is one of the most powerful chapters in all of scripture. It begins with the Pentecostal outpouring of the Holy Spirit on the 120 in the upper room, the birth of the Christian Church. Peter's phenomenal sermon is next. The sermon is followed by the listeners' responses. The chapter ends with the Church growing as followers of Jesus are added daily. These are just the high points in the chapter. There is so much more.

Today we want to focus on preaching and response. A careful reading of Peter's sermon reveals his primary task is to preach Jesus and demonstrate his reliance on Scripture. Further, he calls the listener to be accountable for what is heard. The people, upon hearing the Gospel asked the most natural question: "What must we do?" Peter told them how to respond: "Repent and be baptized..." Three thousand did!

Being filled with the Holy Spirit is necessary for effective living and effective ministry. The Gospel we proclaim in the power of the Holy Spirit is the scriptural witness to the life, death, and resurrection of Jesus. This Gospel demands a response. When the Gospel of Jesus is preached in the power of the Holy Spirit - in faithfulness to the scriptures, lives will be changed. If that is not happening in our churches, what piece(s) of the above is(are) missing?

When we who follow Jesus, live in the power of the fullness of the Holy Spirit, lives are transformed. Are you leading others to a transforming relationship with Jesus?

Thoughts of the day

Prayer list.

1.
2.
3.
4.
5.
6.
7.
8.

Read Acts 3

Then Peter said, "Silver or gold I do not have, but what I do have I give you. In the name of Jesus Christ of Nazareth, walk."* *Acts 3:6.

Two major events occur in this chapter and they are intimately linked: the healing of the lame man at the Temple and the preaching of the gospel of Jesus Christ. Notice that the outpouring of the Holy Spirit promised by Jesus in Chapter 1 and realized by the 120 followers of Jesus in Chapter 2 results in "signs and wonders" and the preaching of the gospel of Jesus in Chapter 3. This first "sign and wonder" was the healing of the lame man.

Jesus had promised his followers they would receive power when they were filled with the Holy Spirit. Notice, he did not say they would be prosperous. Unfortunately, many have swapped the riches of the Spirit for the poverty of materialism. Peter and John had no money, "silver or gold," but they had the power of the Spirit. Most of us, at least in the US, have the riches of "silver and gold," but have no power through the Holy Spirit to do what Peter did at the Temple.

Be Filled With

Be Filled With

While our pulpits give advice on how to live a happy and prosperous life, the power of the Holy Spirit to produce Acts' signs and wonders is almost totally absent. Just listen to our prayer requests. We ask for prayer for sick or dying relatives and friends, but do we hear about miraculous answers to prayer, miraculous signs and wonders?

We have the "silver and gold," but we lack what Peter had: the power of the Holy Spirit to heal the sick, to perform miracles. As we continue to read the Book of Acts, we will see the central role "signs and wonders" played in the spreading of the Gospel to "the ends of the earth." Historically, every great expansion of the Gospel has been accompanied by miraculous "signs and wonders." These miracles give credibility, affirmation, and connection to the gospel being preached.

What is needed today? Repentance and a deep hunger to be filled with the Holy Spirit. Church programs will not produce this. Denominational leadership will not produce this. It isn't produced. It is given. Each individual believer needs to open themselves to accept it. How can you receive it? Desire it. Repent of the self-reliance which prevents the Spirit's control of your life. Surrender every known "idol" of self-will to God's will. Ask God to fill you with the Holy Spirit. Receive the filling of Holy Spirit. Then go with the boldness of Simon Peter to do the work of Jesus and give the witness of Christ.

Thoughts of the day

____

____

____

____

____

____

____

____

Prayer list.

1. ____
2. ____
3. ____
4. ____
5. ____
6. ____
7. ____
8. ____

Read Acts 4

***"Salvation is found in no one else, for there is no other name under heaven given to mankind by which we must be saved."* Acts 4:12**

When called before the religious establishment in Jerusalem, the Apostles Peter and John were said to have been filled with the Holy Spirit as they gave an account of their actions. Peter preached Jesus to them. He preached about Jesus' life, death and resurrection. Notice the impact, the unbelieving religious leaders "took note of them that they had been with Jesus."

The filling of the Holy Spirit in our lives will always be in witness to Jesus. Luke will later refer to the Holy Spirit as the "Spirit of Jesus." It is in the power of the filling of the Holy Spirit that followers of Jesus have the holy boldness to preach the gospel of Jesus. Why is this so important? Because "Salvation is found in no one else, for there is no other name under heaven given to mankind by which we must be saved."

In a world, and often increasingly in the church, where "All roads lead to the same place" and all religions are equally true and where my opinion or "my truth" is of equal value to revealed scripture, the unique nature of the Gospel of Jesus must be proclaimed. In order for the church (you and me) to do this effectively, we must be filled with the Holy Spirit. This gives us the holy boldness to proclaim the great truth of the Gospel: Salvation is in the name of Jesus and "no one else."

The religious rulers in Acts did not like this message. They were offended by this message. They did not accept this message. They sought to destroy those who proclaimed this message, but the message did not change. Salvation is in Jesus and Jesus alone. When filled with the Holy Spirit, followers of Jesus will both reflect the nature of Jesus and boldly proclaim the Good News of salvation in Him – in Him alone.

After Peter and John were released and returned to the other believers, the church prayed: "Stretch out your hand to heal and perform signs and wonders through the name of your holy servant Jesus." After they prayed, the place where they were meeting was shaken. And they were all filled with the Holy Spirit and spoke the word of God boldly. Acts 4:30-31.

Do it again, Lord. Do it now. Do it in me.

Thoughts of the day

Prayer list.

1.
2.
3.
4.
5.
6.
7.
8.

Read Acts 5

Signs and Wonders

"The apostles performed many signs and wonders among the people."
Acts 5:12

The physician, Luke, in writing the Acts of the Apostles, goes to great lengths to tell of the "signs and wonders" performed by the apostles through the power of the Holy Spirit. These signs and wonders almost always resulted in more people coming to faith in Christ.

There are places in the world today where signs and wonders occur frequently and people gather to witness or experience these miraculous events. One of my dear friends, family really, tells of a time in her country when the local hospital brought all their patients to the crusade where they were ministering. All the patients were healed. The hospital was emptied and the local newspaper wrote about this event.

Today in Venezuela some of our dearest friends, colleagues, graduates of the Seminary, regularly perform signs and wonders. And the church is experiencing phenomenal growth. God has even done some of these things when I have laid

Signs and Wonders

hands on folks and prayed for them. There are churches in the US where very often "signs and wonders" are performed and new believers are added to the church.

These signs and wonders have almost always been a part of the work of the Holy Spirit. The testimonies of those healed and delivered result in many new followers of Jesus. However, they are almost never present in the institutional church. Some have even boldly proclaimed, 'The age of miracles is passed." And they are right, in their experience. There is no power of the Holy Spirit to do what was done in Acts, nor what is commonly done in many other places.

The Spirit of God has not changed. The needs of humankind have not changed. What has changed? Luke is clear throughout the Book of Acts to note the work of signs and wonders is the result of the filling of the Holy Spirit. These apostles were not super people, yet they had super power. It was the power of the Holy Spirit.

"Oh Lord, send your power just now, and baptize everyone." The cry of that old Campmeeting song must again become the cry of the church if we are ever going to be able to witness and even perform signs and wonders and again see the Lord adding daily to the church.

Thoughts of the day

Prayer list.

1.
2.
3.
4.
5.
6.
7.
8.

An Anointed Servant

Read Acts 6

"They chose Stephen, a man full of faith and of the Holy Spirit... Now Stephen, a man full of God's grace and power, performed great wonders and signs among the people." ***Acts 6:5b,8***

The need had arisen in the church for some folks to care for the feeding of widows. The Apostles felt they had to devote the selves to "prayer and the ministry of the word." Acts 6:4.

The church selected 7 "seven men from among you who are known to be full of the Spirit and wisdom." Acts 6:3. These seven selected deacons were not simply servers in the soup kitchen. They were ministers of the gospel and were so effective they would even suffer death for the sake of their Lord and the faithfulness and power of their witness to Jesus.

Someone has said, "In the Book of Acts you had to be full of the Holy Spirit even to wait on tables." While this is true, "waiting on tables" was one small aspect of the ministry of these selected by the church. What is the one key requirement for leadership and service in the Book of Acts? It is the filling of the Holy Spirit. What about our church?

Want to lead a mission team? Are you filled with the Holy Spirit?
Want to serve on the Finance Committee? Your CPA credential is not enough. Are you filled with the Holy Spirit?
Want to teach a Sunday School Class? Your degree from a Theological Seminary is not enough. Are you filled with the Holy Spirit?
Want to sing in the choir? Your years at Juilliard are not enough. Are you filled with the Holy Spirit?
Want to serve in the Nursery. Your degree in Early Childhood Education is not enough. Are you filled with the Holy Spirit?
Want to Pastor a church? Your ordination is not enough. Are you filled with the Holy Spirit?

The filling of the Holy Spirit was the common denominator among the leaders of the church in the Book of Acts. This resulted in them performing “signs and wonders” and reaching an ever-growing number of people with the Gospel of Jesus. These signs and wonders were not limited to the Apostles. Anyone filled with the Holy Spirit had this capacity.

Do you? Do I? If not, why not? Seek the filling of the Holy Spirit. Seek it today. Seek it now.

An Anointed Servant

Thoughts of the day

Prayer list.

1.
2.
3.
4.
5.
6.
7.
8.

Read Acts 7

But Stephen...

But Stephen, full of the Holy Spirit... Then he fell on his knees and cried out, "Lord, do not hold this sin against them." When he had said this, he fell asleep. ***Acts 7:8a,60***

The Deacon Stephen was introduced by Dr. Luke in the previous chapter as one of the seven selected leaders to serve the needs of the poor widows in the church. He was notably filled with the Holy Spirit and had a life changing ministry. This resulted in his being arrested in Chapter 6 and executed in Chapter 7. Between the arrest and execution is the thoroughly scriptural sermon of Stephen to his accusers. They did not "feel the love" when he said, "You stiff-necked people! Your hearts and ears are still uncircumcised. You are just like your ancestors: You always resist the Holy Spirit!" Acts 7:51. So they stoned him.

Dr. Luke records this execution of the first Christian martyr. Some statistics say Stephen was the first of over 70 million Christians executed world-wide. Last year alone there were reportedly over 100,000 Christians martyred for their faith. Many of these Christians

But Stephen...

throughout history, and even today, were given the option of renouncing their faith to avoid execution. They did not. Instead, they chose death. How can this be explained? Most of us would do or say anything to save our own lives. Why would Stephen and the 70 million others choose death rather than deny their faith in Jesus? Further, how could they? Could we? Would we?

Dr. Luke continued to tell the story of the church in Acts, showing the reality and necessity of being filled with the Holy Spirit. He was especially precise in repeatedly telling the reader that Stephen was filled with the Holy Spirit. Why? This answers the questions of why and how followers of Jesus would suffer death for the sake of the Gospel.

Back during the Jesus Movement of the 1970's, the question was asked, "If you were charged with being a Christian, would there be enough evidence to convict you?" The answer then and now depended on the filling of the Holy Spirit.

Stephen, charged with being a follower of Jesus, was convicted and executed. He was "full of the Holy Spirit." Are you? Am I?

Thoughts of the day

Prayer list.

1.
2.
3.
4.
5.
6.
7.
8.

Perse cution

Read Acts 8

"On that day a great persecution broke out against the church in Jerusalem, and all except the apostles were scattered throughout Judea and Samaria."

Acts 8:1b

Luke has recorded in the first chapter that when the Holy Spirit was given to the followers of Jesus, they would be witnesses "in Jerusalem, Judea, Samaria and the ends of the earth. Acts 1-8 describes that witness in Jerusalem. Now the story shifts to Judea and Samaria where the witness spread, pushed forward by persecution.

There are at least four constants in his story of the church in Acts. First, the followers of Jesus bore witness to Jesus. Second, effective ministry is empowered by the filling of the Holy Spirit. Third, persecution was a reality from the very beginning of the church. Fourth, signs and wonders accompany the preaching of the gospel of Jesus, also empowered by the Holy Spirit.

Therefore, what was true in Acts 1-7 is also true when the witness moves outside Jerusalem, even to the hated Samaritans. These people were viewed as racially,

Perse cution

morally, and religiously inferior to the Jews. They were deemed unworthy even of conversation with Jews. Jesus radically broke ranks with this prejudice through his encounter with the Samaritan woman at Jacob's Well. Here in Acts, his Jewish followers went into Samaria doing the same ministry they had done in Jerusalem, depending on the same power of the Holy Spirit. Further, the gospel gets shared with the first African convert, the Eunuch from Ethiopia. The gospel of Jesus is clearly for all people, in spite of any racial, cultural, religious divisions.

When the church engages in ministry in the power of the Holy Spirit, the gospel is spread to folks who have never heard it. Preaching the gospel transforms lives and is accompanied by miraculous signs and wonders. Mainline churches in the US, including my own, continue to decline. They fail to reach people where they are. Lives are not transformed, and certainly the signs and wonders of Luke's description are almost non-existent. What is missing? It is the power of the Holy Spirit. And the baptism of the Holy Spirit is the only solution for our church.

Further, like the believers in Samaria, we need to receive the fullness of the Holy Spirit. Seek this filling now. Right now.

Thoughts of the day

Prayer list.

1.
2.
3.
4.
5.
6.
7.
8.

Read Acts 9

Conver ted

Then Ananias went to the house and entered it. Placing his hands on Saul, he said, "Brother Saul, the Lord—Jesus, who appeared to you on the road as you were coming here—has sent me so that you may see again and be filled with the Holy Spirit." Immediately, something like scales fell from Saul's eyes, and he could see again. He got up and was baptized, Acts 9:17,18.

Dr. Luke tells in great detail the story of the conversion of Saul on the road to Damascus. His was a very dramatic conversion. Luke had introduced the reader to Saul back in chapter 7. He was the Pharisee who was in charge at the first martyrdom of a Christian, Stephen. "Meanwhile, the witnesses laid their coats at the feet of a young man named Saul." Acts 7:58b.

Saul was a zealous enforcer for his religion. He had been given authority to travel to Damascus to pursue the followers of Jesus to see that their fate was similar to the fate of Stephen. Saul was well trained, highly educated, passionate, zealous, capable and committed. He was the ideal religious leader, but he did not know Jesus.

Converted

Jesus sought out Saul. The story is told in this chapter, the first of three times Luke would tell it in the next 20 chapters. With the thousands of people who had become followers of Jesus since Pentecost (Chapter 2), why did Luke devote so much space to telling of this one conversion? I believe there were a number of reasons, but among them was the desire to show the extent to which grace will reach and result of that grace applied in a life. Remember, Luke would join Paul later in Macedonia and accompany him during much of his ministry. He saw the ministry of the Holy Spirit both in the transformation of Saul and in his subsequent ministry. Saul became a follower of Jesus and was filled with the Holy Spirit.

Today, the Lord desires to do for each of us what he did for Saul. We can be converted, we can be filled with the Holy Spirit, and we can have a transformational ministry. However, this story is not just for us. It tells us that no matter how much one may be an enemy of the Gospel, the Gospel still has the power to transform their life. Conversion and the filling of the Holy Spirit is possible for "the chief of sinners" as Saul described himself.

This is the Good News we get to tell to someone today. Will we tell it? Do we believe it? Have we experienced it?

Thoughts of the day

Prayer list.

1.
2.
3.
4.
5.
6.
7.
8.

The Gospel is Given to the Gentiles

Read Acts 10

***"While Peter was still speaking these words, the Holy Spirit came on all who heard the message."* Acts 10:44**

This entire chapter is testimony to the amazing grace of Jesus reaching out to those who need the salvation only available in Christ. The big story here is the Gospel is given to the Gentiles. It is not just for the Jews.

In telling the "big story", Luke weaves in several smaller stories - each of particular significance. One is about the Centurion, Cornelius. He was a godly, generous man, and devout in his faith, but he needed Jesus. Another smaller story was Peter's religious and cultural superiority preventing him from even considering taking the gospel to the Gentiles. Another story is God's work in Peter's life to break down his cultural and religious barriers. Another smaller story is how the Lord spoke to both Cornelius and Peter and both were obedient to that which was revealed to them. There are other smaller stories within the greater story.

Peter preached the life, death, and resurrection to the people at the house of Cornelia, and a surprising thing happened. "While Peter was still speaking these words, the Holy Spirit came on all who heard the message." This was not supposed to happen to Gentiles, not in Peter's world. But God broke the ethnic and religious barrier as the Holy Spirit came on all who heard the message. Notice this occurred while Peter was preaching Jesus. The work of the Holy Spirit is to glorify Jesus and reproduce his nature in our lives. And this work extended to the Gentiles in the house of Cornelius.

Who are the folks today who are waiting, maybe even longing to hear the Gospel of Jesus Christ? What are the barriers which keep us from sharing the Good News? Can the Holy Spirit move us out of our places of comfort and complacency to reach the world with the Gospel?

I've been privileged to see the Holy Spirit poured out on many different people in many places around the world. I am praying to see it again in my home country in ways never experienced before. Come, Holy Spirit.

The Gospel is Given to the Gentiles

Thoughts of the day

Prayer list.

1.
2.
3.
4.
5.
6.
7.
8.

Read Acts 11

"As I began to speak, the Holy Spirit came on them as he had come on us at the beginning. Then I remembered what the Lord had said: 'John baptized with water, but you will be baptized with the Holy Spirit So if God gave them the same gift he gave us who believed in the Lord Jesus Christ, who was I to think that I could stand in God's way?"

Acts 11:15-17.

Only One Requirement

Luke continues the story of the Acts of the Apostles keeping the consistent link to the filling of the Holy Spirit in the birth and growth of the church. First, the quote above is from Peter as he recounts what happened in Chapter 10 at the house of the Roman Centurion, Cornelius.

Then we hear of the gospel spreading to other areas, in particular Antioch. The leaders of the church in Jerusalem sent Barnabas to Antioch to lead the church there. "He was a good man, full of the Holy Spirit and faith, and a great number of people were brought to the Lord." Acts 11:24

Notice the growth of the church is intentionally connected by Luke to a

Only One
Requirement

person "full of the Holy Spirit..." Further, Barnabas recruited the young Christian, Saul, the former persecutor of the church, to join him in the work in Antioch. Luke places this decision directly within the context of being full of the Holy Spirit. That is then followed by the ministry of a prophet (one of the specific gifts and callings of the Holy Spirit, Paul would later write about). The prophesy resulted in an offering being taken for the church in Jerusalem during the historically documented prophesied famine.

The truth is Luke went to great pains to tell the story of the birth and growth of the church as outlined in Acts 1:8, all within the central theme of "being full of the Holy Spirit."

Why are all the tremendous things the Apostles do, Acts, recorded by Luke tied to the filling of the Holy Spirit? Someone once said the church gave the wrong title to Luke's book. It was not the Acts of the Apostles, but would have been more accurate naming it "The Acts of the Holy Spirit."

Need miracles? Need prophesies? Need barriers broken. Need generosity developed? Need to reach the lost? Need to spread the gospel across racial, religious, national and cultural boundaries? Need to see the full exercise of the work of the Holy Spirit? Need to see folks converted?

Be filled with the Holy Spirit.

Thoughts of the day

____
____
____
____
____
____
____
____

Prayer list.

1. ____
2. ____
3. ____
4. ____
5. ____
6. ____
7. ____
8. ____

Read Acts 12

***"But the word of God continued to spread and flourish."* Acts 12:24**

This chapter continues the story of the persecution of the church, led by Herod and supported by the Jewish leaders. Herod had executed James, the brother of John. He had imprisoned Peter and intended the same fate for him.

But the church prayed, and the Lord sent an angel to deliver Peter from prison. Here we have one of the great dilemmas of the faith. Why is Peter miraculously delivered and James was not?

I do not have the answer. This is when I have to trust in the nature of God as revealed in Jesus, and not my own very limited understanding of the acts of God. I do know God sees clearly while I see "through a glass darkly." As my preacher son reminded me last night, I want a god of my own creation instead of the God of creation. I can manage, control, even manipulate the god of my creation. I cannot do that with the God of creation. His ways are far above my ways. I can only surrender to the God of Creation, or reject him for an idol, the god of my creation.

James is executed. Peter is delivered. King Herod dies an ugly death. For what end?

"But the word of God continued to spread and flourish." The Acts of the Apostles was written to continue the story of Jesus which Luke had written in his first book also addressed to Theophilus. Acts was written to tell what happened when the promised Holy Spirit was given to the followers of Jesus. This was the exponential growth of the church, even in very adversarial circumstances.

We may not understand or grasp it all. Our theology may be incomplete, even unsophisticated. But God continues to do the work of redemption of the lost through the ministry of those followers of Jesus who have been filled with the Holy Spirit. If people are not being converted and the church is not growing, according to the Book of Acts, it is because we have not done what those followers of Jesus did: be filled with the Holy Spirit. When the followers of Jesus are filled with the Holy Spirit, the church grows, the word of God flourishes.

Is my life bearing the fruit of one filled with the Holy Spirit? Am I seeing the word of God flourishing? If not, why not? What must I do?

Thoughts of the day

____
____
____
____
____
____
____
____

Prayer list.

1. ______________________________________
2. ______________________________________
3. ______________________________________
4. ______________________________________
5. ______________________________________
6. ______________________________________
7. ______________________________________
8. ______________________________________

Read Acts 13

***"And the disciples were filled with joy and with the Holy Spirit."* Acts 13:52**

Are You Filled?

When the chapter and verse designations were done in the Book of Acts, long after Luke had written it, they missed the fact that verse 25 of Chapter 12, really should have been verse 1 of Chapter 13,

"When Barnabas and Saul had finished their mission, they returned from Jerusalem, taking with them John, also called Mark." Acts 13:2.

Barnabas and Saul had been pastoring the church in Antioch. They took the offering of the church back to Jerusalem to help with famine relief. They returned, bringing with them the young John Mark.

As they were worshipping at Antioch, the Holy Spirit spoke to the church telling them to set apart Barnabas and Saul "for the work to which I have called them." The church sent them on their first missionary journey. They went to people who had never heard the Gospel of Jesus and they preached and performed signs and wonders. And it was all done in the power of the Holy Spirit. As these new

Are You Filled?

believers, these new followers of Jesus began their spiritual journey, they were "filled with joy and with the Holy Spirit." It was the same as what the followers of Jesus experienced on Pentecost, in Acts 2.

As Luke tells his story of the work - the birth, the ministry, and growth of the church - he continues to emphasize it is all through the power of the filling of the Holy Spirit. Only Spirit filled people are equipped and empowered to do Kingdom work. The institutional church does not require the filling of the Holy Spirit to do church work, whether as a Bishop or an usher. We can do the work of the institutional church in our own power. I have done it and so have so many others.

The work of the Kingdom requires the filling of the Holy Spirit. Have you been filled with the Holy Spirit? Are you filled with the Holy Spirit? If not, why not and why not now?

Thoughts of the day

Prayer list.

1.
2.
3.
4.
5.
6.
7.
8.

Bold ness

Read Acts 14

"So Paul and Barnabas spent considerable time there, speaking boldly for the Lord, who confirmed the message of his grace by enabling them to perform signs and wonders."

Acts 14:3

In this verse there are two very significant results of the filling of the Holy Spirit as described by Luke: boldness to speak the word of the Lord, and signs and wonders which confirm the message of the Gospel of Jesus Christ.

Personal testimony: I was filled with the Holy Spirit in February, 1972. The one clear impact in my life that was so very obvious to me was boldness. Timidity had been the mark of my Christianity, my experience of grace. I knew I was a believer, but I lacked holy boldness. That changed instantaneously. Further, along the way I began to see signs and wonders that bore testimony to the word spoken boldly. But as a confession, I did not see the number of signs and wonders I should have due to my own inadequate faith.

Do you have the holy Boldness to speak the gospel in every situation and opportunity? Do you see signs and wonders as confirmation of the word of witness to Jesus?

The church grows in new ways and new places when spirit filled followers of Jesus speak the word of God with boldness. That testimony is confirmed by signs and wonders. It has happened in every revival movement in the history of the church. It happens today in those places in the world where spirit-filled followers of Jesus speak the word of God with boldness, and His word is confirmed by miraculous signs and wonders.

This is what is required for our nation to be saved from the spiritual depravity so prevalent in our society. When this happens, the church will grow again and lives will be changed. Strategies and programs and marketing cannot do this. It will only happen when followers of Jesus experience the filling of the Holy Spirit, speak the word of God with boldness, and perform miraculous signs and wonders. Then they will take knowledge of us that we have been with Jesus.

Thoughts of the day

Prayer list.

1.
2.
3.
4.
5.
6.
7.
8.

Read Acts 15

Conflicts and Solutions

"They had such a sharp disagreement that they parted company."

Acts 15:39

The 15th Chapter of Acts is primarily about two very contentious issues, or conflicts, and how they are resolved. The first is the conflict concerning the necessity of Jewish religious law and its imposition on Gentile believers. This was resolved in what is known as the Jerusalem Council. The Gentiles were not required to observe Jewish laws, but were to refrain from eating meat offered to idols and sexual immorality. The second major conflict was between Barnabas and Saul. It was over a "personnel issue". Barnabas wanted to take John Mark with them on their second missionary journey. Saul did not want him along since he had deserted them during the first missionary journey. Luke describes their disagreement as a "sharp disagreement." It was so fierce, they went their separate ways.

Lessons:

1.Conflict in the church is unavoidable. It will come. Therefore, it is imperative the church learn how to resolve the conflict in productive, God honoring ways.

Conflicts and Solutions

2.Conflict in itself is not a bad thing. It is not necessarily the result of sin. People simply see and understand things from a different perspective.

3.Conflict is not the result of the absence of the Holy Spirit working in the church. Luke carefully records that all the parties in both of the conflicts in Acts 15 were full of the Holy Spirit and signs and wonders validated their ministries.

4.Conflict resolution can result in greater unity, as was the case with the Gentile believers.

5.Conflict can result in even greater division, as was the case with Barnabas and Saul.

6.Conflict can be used by God to further the work of the Kingdom. Both conflicts in this chapter resulted in greater ministry. I have never been involved in any church that did not experience conflict. Some learned to resolve it in God honoring ways. Others did not resolve it and moved deeper and deeper into dysfunction.

My denomination has been in the national news lately regarding the conflict currently dividing our church. Much of what we have done has been a result of our inability to resolve the conflict. Hence, we have moved further and further into the morass of dysfunction. Our last General Conference in February of 2019 was an embarrassment to the Kingdom. Our next General Conference in May has the opportunity to resolve the conflict. Most of us believe the only healthy and God-honoring way to do this is the way Barnabas and Saul resolved their conflict over John Mark. They split, and both went on a second missionary journey, but in separate directions. Their ministries continued in the power of the Holy Spirit.

There are times in the church when separation is the only solution to the conflict. We are at that place in our denomination. This will impact every local church in the denomination, forcing them to make a very difficult decision. They will have to decide whether to accompany Barnabas or Saul. Every member of the congregation will essentially have to make that same decision. The Holy Spirit is present in the conflict even when the decision is to separate. There are times when this is the only good decision. Conflict forces us to decide on what is really important.

It breaks the inertia of indecision. It clarifies a new direction and a new way of living out our calling. Embrace it. Learn the healthy ways of resolving conflict. This will result in even greater work in the Kingdom.

Thoughts of the day

____
____
____
____
____
____
____
____

Prayer list.

1. ______________________________________
2. ______________________________________
3. ______________________________________
4. ______________________________________
5. ______________________________________
6. ______________________________________
7. ______________________________________
8. ______________________________________

Read Acts 16

They replied, "Believe in the Lord Jesus, and you will be saved —you and your household." Acts 16:31

Believe...and You Will Be Saved

The message of the gospel is the story of salvation in Jesus Christ. The whole of Scripture, all 66 Books, is the story of salvation. It began in Genesis in the Garden of Eden when God created Adam and Eve in his own image. They sinned, the image was marred, and original sin was passed on to every subsequent generation. The rest of Scripture tells of God's gracious acts to redeem lost humanity. This culminates in the life, death, and resurrection of Jesus. Through his atoning death and resurrection, all of humankind can be saved.

Paul and Silas, now accompanied by Luke and Timothy, were traveling around the Mediterranean preaching this gospel of salvation in Jesus. Many were coming to faith in Jesus. Then Paul and Silas were arrested, beaten, and thrown in prison in chains for preaching the Gospel. An earthquake shook the prison, their chains fell off, and the doors were opened. The jailer, thinking the prisoners had escaped, was about to commit suicide, when Paul

Believe...and You Will Be Saved

reassured him they were all still inside the prison. The jailer then asked the question, "What must I do to be saved?"

The answer is so very simple, "Believe in the Lord Jesus, and you will be saved —you and your household." He and his household did so, were saved, and then baptized. Can it be that simple? Don't we have to do something besides believe in the Lord Jesus? Repent? Clean up our lives? Study the catechism? Give away our money? Get married? Apparently all that is required for salvation is believing in the Lord Jesus. How can this be? It is the story of amazing grace. God's unmerited favor is bestowed on us whereby we can be saved.

Paul and Silas devoted their lives sharing the good news of salvation in Jesus with unbelievers. That is still the task of the church. When we share the gospel, people are saved if they believe in the Lord Jesus.

What must you do to be saved? Believe in the Lord Jesus and you will be saved.

Thoughts of the day

Prayer list.

1.
2.
3.
4.
5.
6.
7.
8.

Read Acts 17

A group of Epicurean and Stoic philosophers began to debate with him. Some of them asked, "What is this babbler trying to say?" Others remarked, "He seems to be advocating foreign gods." They said this because Paul was preaching the good news about Jesus and the resurrection.

Acts 17:18

First, notice in this chapter that everywhere Paul traveled, he preached the Gospel of Jesus: in Thessolonica, in Berea, in Athens. Notice also the preaching of the gospel was met with joyful acceptance as well as with significant opposition, the most venomous of which was from the religious leaders. The secular philosophers, the intelligencia of Athens, also questioned the veracity of his preaching calling it "babble." Paul was consistent in preaching the "good news about Jesus and the resurrection." In this, he provides the pattern for all Christian preaching.

I have been preaching since 1972. I have taught preaching in a variety of settings since 1984. I have read and observed literally hundreds of sermons in classrooms, on video, and through service on the Board of Ministry. One of the questions I learned to ask was, "Where is Christ in this sermon?" Where is the life, atoning death and resurrection of Jesus in the sermon?

It is possible to preach many eloquent, even helpful, sermons but miss preaching Jesus. One can preach for a year from the Book of Psalms and never preach the gospel of Jesus. Sermons on the ethical and moral teachings of Jesus can be quite enlightening, but never declare gospel. The Major and Minor prophets have much to say that can be very helpful, but one can preach from them for a lifetime and never preach the Gospel of Jesus. What about the Wisdom of Proverbs or the great biblical stories in the Pentateuch and the Historical Books? This is great material, however, one can write wonderful sermons from those texts and never preach Jesus.

Hence, the questions: "Where is Christ in this sermon, Where is the gospel?" Preaching that fails to declare the nature and work of Jesus, incarnation, atoning death, and resurrection is not Christian preaching. All of the scriptures are written to bring Jesus and the story of salvation to our attention.

Good Rews of Resurrection

When the Gospel is preached, Jesus is declared - his life, his death and his resurrection. And people do one of two things when they hear the gospel. 1. They embrace it and are saved. 2. They reject it and are lost. Preachers are not responsible for the response people choose. But we are fully responsible to preach the Gospel with such clarity the listeners are forced to make some response. Tragically, so much of what passes for preaching in the church does not require any response by the listener.

We have good news to tell! It doesn't matter if it is from the pulpit of a high steeple church , the sacred desk of a humble meeting house, a house church sitting on the ground, or even the breakroom at work. We must share the "good news about Jesus and the resurrection".

Thoughts of the day

Prayer list.

1.
2.
3.
4.
5.
6.
7.
8.

The Ultimate Price

Read Acts 18

Then the crowd there turned on Sosthenes the synagogue leader and beat him in front of the proconsul; and Gallio showed no concern whatever.

Acts 18:17

Persecution has been a regular companion to those who carry the gospel to unbelievers. Throughout the Book of Acts, as the gospel spreads "from Jerusalem to Judea to Samaria and to the ends of the earth" as Jesus foretold, persecution was part of the price the believers paid.

Scholars place this event some 20-25 years after Pentecost. Across those years, people like Paul, Barnabas,Silas , Timothy, Pricilla, and Aquila planted churches while enduring persecution. Yesterday, a fellow Christian wrote on his FaceBook wall that Muslims attacked him and threw rocks at him for preaching the Gospel. Today there are Christians who are having to meet in caves in secret because of the fear of death. In Africa, India, North Korea, China, and many other countries, preaching Jesus is dangerous, even deadly.

The Ultimate Price

These Christians keep preaching, keep telling the Good News of Jesus, knowing at any time they could be killed for their faith. Like Sosthenes, they are willing to pay any price necessary to follow Jesus and share his love with the lost. Their testimony makes any hardship I have ever suffered for the gospel pale in comparison. In fact, there is no comparison. I have no broken bones. I have no physical scars. I've never had to meet with fellow followers of Jesus in secret out of fear of death. Thank God others have been willing to pay the ultimate price to share the Gospel of Jesus.

"He is no fool to give up what he cannot keep for what he cannot lose," wrote Jim Elliot while he was preparing to become a missionary. He was killed by the Indians in Ecuador in 1956 in his attempt to share the gospel with them. Today we have friends serving in Ecuador who have regular contact with that indigenous tribe which was converted by those who followed the martyrs into those same jungles.

Oh God, give me the kind of passion for the gospel of Jesus that I would willingly put everything on the line for the sake of the Him.

See:
https://www.opendoorsusa.org/christian-persecution/stories/the-10-most-dangerous-places-for-christians/?utm_campaign=coschedule&utm_source=facebook_page&utm_medium=Open%20Doors%20USA

Thoughts of the day

Prayer list.

1.
2.
3.
4.
5.
6.
7.
8.

Read Acts 19

While Apollos was at Corinth, Paul took the road through the interior and arrived at Ephesus. There he found some disciples and asked them,"Diid you receive the Holy Spirit when you believed?"

They answered,"No, we have not even heard that there is a Holy Spirit."

Acts 19:1,2

Apollos was a Jewish preacher of Jesus, "a learned man with a thorough knowledge of the scriptures." Of course, when Luke wrote that, the only scriptures were what we know as the Old Testament. He did not know the full gospel of Jesus and only preached repentance, "the baptism of John." Apparently, he was a very effective preacher since he left in his wake at Ephesus believers in Jesus. However, their experience with Christ was incomplete. They had not been filled with the Holy Spirit. When they were baptized by Paul and he laid hands on them ,they received the Holy Spirit and one of the gifts of the Spirit: speaking in tongues.

I was born again when I was eight years old, but I was not filled with the Spirit

Did You Receive the Holy Spirit?

Did You Receive the Holy Spirit?

until I was 19. I only became aware of the possibility or desirability of being filled with the Spirit when I was 18, followed by a year of seeking to understand this reality and get my life and faith to align with the Lord's will for me.

I do not blame the church or pastors or teachers for not telling me about the necessity of being filled with the Holy Spirit. Some of them were the most Spirit filled people I have ever known. I simply was not attuned to the message that Paul shared with the believers at Ephesus. However, when I gradually became aware of both my need to be filled and the potential to be filled, a hunger was created in me by the grace of Jesus that could not be satisfied by anything else. Then in February, 1972 in a prayer meeting in a living room, the Holy Spirit was poured out on me and everything changed!

Methodists have referred to this as a second work of grace. The filling of the Holy Spirit results in holiness of heart and life, inward and outward holiness. This sanctification, which is initiated at the new birth, progresses in our lives through the work of the Holy Spirit. It is the experience of many believers that after their conversion there is a second, often dramatic, work of grace resulting in being filled with the Holy Spirit. Effectiveness in Holy living depends on the work of the Holy Spirit in one's life. Effective witness to Jesus and effective ministry depends on the work of the Holy Spirit.

I ask you what Paul asked the believers at Ephesus, "Did you receive the Holy Spirit when you believed?" Your answer must be validated by your experience, not by what you have believed or been taught by others concerning the Holy Spirit. Do you see the same impact in your life which the Spirit had on the church In Acts?

If your spirit does not leap in affirmation, seek now to be filled with the Holy Spirit. Read Acts in one sitting every day for a week. Study the Epistles of Paul. Read what Jesus said about the Spirit in the Gospel of John. Seek the filling of the Holy Spirit until it happens. God desires to give you the Spirit. God is faithful.

Did You Receive the Holy Spirit?

Thoughts of the day

Prayer list.

1.
2.
3.
4.
5.
6.
7.
8.

Read Acts 20

The Value of Life

However, I consider my life worth nothing to me; my only aim is to finish the race and complete the task the Lord Jesus has given me —the task of testifying to the good news of God's grace. ***Acts 20:24***

What is your life worth? Paul had placed the value of his life precisely where it needed to be: "worth nothing to me." His life's worth was not to himself, but only as he gave himself to completing the "task the Lord Jesus has given me."

Paul understood the nature of being a follower of Jesus, "If you would be my disciple, you must deny yourself and follow me." Further, Jesus said, "If you want to find your life, you must lose it." This is not easy chair or padded pew religion. This is not the way of powering through to a majority vote in the church to get what I want. This is not bumper sticker discipleship. This is life and death.

Paul likens his life to being in a race. No matter the difficulty, his only goal was to finish. The serious competitive runner in a race only sees the finish line - the goal. The crowds mean nothing to him.

The Value of Life

The other runners are only significant if they are between him and his goal. Paul's race was not a marathon or a 5-K, it was "testifying to the good news of God's grace." This task would require him to leave his friends at Ephesus, go to Jerusalem, be arrested for his faith, and demand a trial before Caesar so he could preach the Gospel in Rome. He understood his might be a one-way trip. Hence his word to the leaders from Ephesus that he would not see them again.

Paul could see the rest of the course all the way to the finish line. Therefore, his life only had value if he completed the race - the task the Lord had given him. His renown as a preacher, missionary, healer, and miracle worker was of no significance to Paul compared to the importance of finishing the race and completing the task of testifying to the grace of Jesus.

What is the value of your life? Is it measured in dollars in your 401-K? Is it measured in the number of grandchildren you have? Is it in the trophies you have accumulated along the way? Is it the titles you wear?

The only thing worth a life is the "task the Lord Jesus has given me." When that task is defined as "testifying to the good news of God's grace," how much is your life worth?

Like Paul, I want to count my life as of no value, and completing the task the Lord has given me to be of the ultimate value... even if it costs me my life. However, that is no great cost since "I consider my life worth nothing to me..."

Thoughts of the day

____
____
____
____
____
____
____
____

Prayer list.

1. ______________________________________
2. ______________________________________
3. ______________________________________
4. ______________________________________
5. ______________________________________
6. ______________________________________
7. ______________________________________
8. ______________________________________

A Team in the Spirit

Read Acts 21

Leaving the next day, we reached Caesarea and stayed at the house of Philip the evangelist, one of the Seven. He had four unmarried daughters who prophesied. ***Acts 21:8.***

In this one paragraph, three of the five offices of ministry as Paul defined them appear: Apostle (Paul), Evangelist (Philip - a Deacon) and Prophet, four daughters of Phillip. Paul would list these and the other offices of ministry in Ephesians 4:11f: "So Christ himself gave the apostles, the prophets, the evangelists, the pastors and teachers, to equip his people for works of service, so that the body of Christ may be built up until we all reach unity in the faith and in the knowledge of the Son of God and become mature, attaining to the whole measure of the fullness of Christ."

All five of these need to be functioning in the body for there to be maturity and unity in the faith. Paul describes spiritual maturity as "attaining to the whole measure of the fullness of Christ." The church in Acts was blessed with all five offices of ministry functioning together to complete the work of Christ. Unity in the faith and spiritual maturity are the result.

A Team in the Spirit

Unfortunately, I spent most of my ministry in an ecclesiastical system which essentially limited the offices of ministry to Pastor and teacher. Some would say our Bishops are apostles, but that does not meet the primary roles for Apostles in the New Testament. We used to recognize the office of Evangelist and value it, but over the life of my denomination we have minimized this office until it basically does not exist for us. The office of Prophet, we have completely ignored.

I must ask why this has occurred? Why do we only really have the office of Pastor and Teacher? Then it occurs to me, one can do the work of a pastor or a teacher in one's own strength, rather than in the power of the Holy Spirit. The work of an Apostle accompanied with "signs and wonders, the work of Evangelist with large numbers of new followers of Jesus, and the work of a Prophet speaking revealed truth into contemporary circumstance as well as speaking a word for the future, all depend on the Holy Spirit. While one can be a Pastor or Teacher without the working of the Spirit, one cannot be an

A Team in the Spirit

Apostle, Evangelist or Prophet without the Spirit at work through being filled with the Holy Spirit.

Now it makes sense why so many of our churches are shrinking and dying instead of being built up, why we lack the spiritual maturity of which Paul speaks, and why our growth in holiness (the whole measure of Christ) is so stunted. We need to be filled with the Holy Spirit.

Effective ministry depends on the fullness of the Holy Spirit. Many pastors and teachers in my church will be offended by this. Unless one sees the growth of the church as it occurs in Acts in our churches, we cannot claim to filled with the Holy Spirit. We will never be effective as Apostles, Prophets, and Evangelists apart from the fullness of the Spirit.

Jesus said, "Likewise, every good tree bears good fruit, but a bad tree bears bad fruit. A good tree cannot bear bad fruit, and a bad tree cannot bear good fruit. Every tree that does not bear good fruit is cut down and thrown into the fire. Thus, by their fruit you will recognize them." Matthew 7:17f.

As the Mainline churches in the US continue their rapid decline and ineffectiveness, what is the obvious conclusion from reading Acts? We have not done what Jesus told his followers to do: "...but wait for the gift my Father promised, which you have heard me speak about. For John baptized with water, but in a few days, you will be baptized with the Holy Spirit." Acts 4:4bf. When that occurs, the result in the church will be the result we see in Acts. I pray and cry for this for the church in the US. Will you join me?

Thoughts of the day

____
____
____
____
____
____
____
____

Prayer list.

1. ______________________________
2. ______________________________
3. ______________________________
4. ______________________________
5. ______________________________
6. ______________________________
7. ______________________________
8. ______________________________

Let Him Transform Your Life

Read Acts 22

I studied under Gamaliel and was thoroughly trained in the law of our ancestors. I was just as zealous for God as any of you are today. Acts 22:3b

Luke had previously written of Paul's experience of conversion. Now Paul tells it in the first person here in the 22nd chapter. Three times it is recorded in Acts. Therefore, Luke, in writing this book of just 28 chapters, deemed it of great significance.

Much of the Book of Acts tells about Saul who presided at the stoning of Stephen, the first Christian martyr. In this testimony, he reiterates his religious training, his zealousness, and his heritage. He was fully committed to his "Tribe".

When he was converted on the road to Damascus, he did not simply change religions. No, what happened there was far more significant. Yes, the one who persecuted the followers of "The Way" became one of them, but more happened than a transactional change from one belief system to another. Paul was transformed by his encounter with Jesus. This is what Jesus was talking about when he said to another Pharisee named Nicodemus,

"You must be born again." John 3.

The transformation Jesus performs in a life is so profound the only adequate way to describe it, even for the Lord of Creation, is to describe it as a "new birth." Too much of our Protestant religious experience of "believing in Jesus" has been a religious transaction. The Lord desires to transform us like he did Paul. That can only be accomplished through a work of the Holy Spirit as Jesus said to Nicodemus.

Have you been transformed? Has the Spirit done the work in you that Jesus spoke of and to which Pail testified? He will. Seek him now. Let him transform your life.

Thoughts of the day

____
____
____
____
____
____
____
____

Prayer list.

1. ____________________________
2. ____________________________
3. ____________________________
4. ____________________________
5. ____________________________
6. ____________________________
7. ____________________________
8. ____________________________

Legacy of faith

Read Acts 23

Then he ordered that Paul be kept under guard in Herod's palace.

Acts 23:35b

The Apostle Paul had suffered a great deal for the sake of the gospel. Beatings, imprisonments, tortures, deprivation, and more were a part of his faithful service to Christ. Yet he was able to be faithful in these difficult circumstances.

Luke records:

"Paul looked straight at the Sanhedrin and said, 'My brothers, I have fulfilled my duty to God in all good conscience to this day'." Acts 23:1.

The difficulties did not go away. After beatings and a plot to assassinate him in Jerusalem, he was taken as a prisoner to Caesarea by the Sea. He was placed under the protection of Governor Felix while he awaited trial. He was housed in the luxurious palace of Herod. However, his accommodations were probably not in the luxury section!

The hardships Paul endured allowed him to have opportunity to share the Gospel with people who would never seek to hear the Good News of Jesus. We will see this is the case in the next chapter.

Legacy of faith

I have had the privilege of visiting the ruins of the great palace of Herod the Great in Caesarea. The ruins are quite impressive and the location is beautiful - on the beach of the Mediterranean Sea. Alas, they are just ruins. They and similar ruins are all that remain of the Great Herod.

Paul's testimony given in that palace and in many other places lives on. It inspires millions of Christians in lands rife with the persecution of Christians. His testimony strengthens the whole church when traversing through times of difficulty and suffering.

Why is Herod the Great essentially forgotten by history and the witness of a Jewish prisoner, Paul, housed in Herod's palace so alive and inspiring? It is because Paul "fulfilled my duty to God."

Paul was called to take the Gospel to the Gentiles. Most of us reading this today who follow Jesus owe a great debt of gratitude to the Apostle Paul who faithfully executed his call.

What will remain after we are gone? It

won't be houses and wealth. They will disappear rather quickly. All that will remain is what we have done to "fulfill our duty to God," to live out our calling. If we do that, there will most likely be times of suffering, opposition, and deprivation. Just think about where our faithfulness can take us! Think about the legacy of faith we will leave for others.

Paul seized the opportunity in suffering to be faithful to his call. Today we give thanks.

Thoughts of the day

____
____
____
____
____
____
____
____

Prayer list.

1. ______________________________________
2. ______________________________________
3. ______________________________________
4. ______________________________________
5. ______________________________________
6. ______________________________________
7. ______________________________________
8. ______________________________________

Read Acts 24

Several days later Felix came with his wife Drusilla, who was Jewish. He sent for Paul and listened to him as he spoke about faith in Christ Jesus. As Paul talked about righteousness, self-control and the judgment to come, Felix was afraid and said, "That's enough for now! You may leave. When I find it convenient, I will send for you."

Acts 24:24,25

Back when Methodists believed in altar calls, one of the most plaintive hymns we would sing inviting a response to the Gospel of Jesus said:
Almost persuaded now to believe;
Almost persuaded Christ to receive;
Seems now some soul to say,
'Go, Spirit, go Thy way,
Some more convenient day
on Thee I'll call.'

This song was based on this passage in Acts and another coming later. Felix gave Paul several opportunities to share the gospel with him. However, he rejected the gospel stating he would pursue it further when it was more "convenient." It appears it never became "convenient" for Felix to become one of the followers of "The Way."

Following Jesus is Inconvenient

Following Jesus has never been convenient. If your religion is convenient, you are not following Jesus.

It was not convenient for Peter and Andrew to quit fishing to follow Jesus.
It was not convenient for Mary, Martha, and Lazarus to follow a Jesus.
It was not convenient for Zaccheus to follow Jesus.
It was not convenient for Stephen to follow Jesus.

This is why Jesus said, "In the same way, those of you who do not give up everything you have cannot be my disciples." Luke 14:33.

That doesn't sound too convenient, does it? However, church membership, even Christianity has been so domesticated as to become simply convenient. Our consumer mentality causes us to reject any demand of the Gospel we find inconvenient. We love our Convenience Stores because they are, well, just so convenient. We love our online shopping and at-home free delivery because it is just so convenient. Following Jesus? It's just not convenient right now.

Feed the hungry? Not convenient.
Welcome the alien and stranger? Not convenient.

Give up my job to follow the Lord's call on my life? Not convenient.
Go to a foreign country as a missionary? Not convenient.
Tithe? Not convenient.
Read my Bible? Not convenient.
Pray for the lost? Not convenient.
Visit the sick? Not convenient.
Go to the prison? Not convenient.
Love the unlovable? Not convenient.
Forgive those who harm me? Not convenient.
Share the Gospel with my neighbors? Not convenient.

Some of us even reject the Lord himself, because like Felix, it's just not convenient. Hell will host a lot of folks who just never could find it convenient to become a follower of The Way. Some of them will be those who always intended to "someday," but it just never became convenient.

Following Jesus is inconvenient. Just ask Paul. It sure beats the alternative.

Thoughts of the day

Prayer list.

1.
2.
3.
4.
5.
6.
7.
8.

Read Acts 25

"Instead, they had some points of dispute with him about their own religion and about a dead man named Jesus who Paul claimed was alive." Acts 25:19

Paul has been imprisoned in Caesarea for about 2 years. He has stood before Felix and Festus. He will soon face Agrippa. The Jews who had charged Paul with a crime came to Caesarea to present their case to Festus. Festus then reported the issue to King Agrippa in this way: "Instead, they had some points of dispute with him about their own religion and about a dead man named Jesus who Paul claimed was alive."

This is the issue: "a dead man named Jesus who Paul claimed was alive." That was the issue with Paul. It was the issue with the Jews. It became the issue with the governors and a King. This is the central issue of the Christian faith. We claim "a dead man named Jesus...was (is) alive." The death and resurrection of Jesus is the key doctrinal and theological claim of our faith. It is so critical that a belief system that does not claim the atoning death and bodily resurrection of Jesus cannot even claim to be Christian.

Paul Claimed He Was Alive

Paul Claimed He Was Alive

However, today in my own denominational colleges and seminaries there are theologians and professors who deny the resurrection of Jesus, and many reject the whole idea of his atoning death. There are denominational leaders who follow their teaching. The Christian faith proclaims the atoning death and resurrection of Jesus or it has nothing to proclaim. People are martyred for the faith somewhere in the world almost every day because they make the same claim Paul made.

We affirm in the Apostle's Creed, "I believe in Jesus Christ, his only son our Lord, who was conceived by the Holy Spirit, born of the Virgin, Mary, suffered under Pontus Pilate, was crucified, dead and buried, the third day he rose from the dead..."

I conducted a funeral yesterday for a former church member who was called to preach and went on to pastor several churches. What is the claim we made in that funeral? "A dead man named Jesus... was alive!"

Jesus himself said,
"I am the resurrection and the life. The one who believes in me will live, even

though they die; and whoever lives by believing in me will never die. Do you believe this?" (John 11:25–26)

This is our claim. This is our hope. This is our faith. "A dead man named Jesus" ... is alive! That is worth living for. It is even worth dying for.

Thoughts of the day

____

____

____

____

____

____

____

____

Prayer list.

1. ____
2. ____
3. ____
4. ____
5. ____
6. ____
7. ____
8. ____

Read Acts 26

"I am sending you to them to open their eyes and turn them from darkness to light, and from the power of Satan to God, so that they may receive forgiveness of sins and a place among those who are sanctified by faith in me."

Acts 17b,18

Paul was given the opportunity to witness to his faith and share his testimony with Agrippa, Festus, and their wives. One thought he was crazy. The other thought it incredulous that Paul would think he could convert him in such a short time. Paul, as he would say, was not disobedient to the heavenly vision given to him. It was a vision leading to a faithful witness to both Jews and Gentiles.

The result of Paul's faithfulness to the heavenly vision would be converting unbelievers to faith in Christ. This would result in

1.*Their eyes being opened.*
2.*Turning them from darkness to light,*
3.*Turning them from the power of Satan to God,*
4.*So that they may receive forgiveness of sins and a place among those who are sanctified by faith in Jesus.*

This passage tells us that unregenerate sinners, a condition we are all born into, are blind to spiritual truth, they live in darkness, in the power of Satan. My wife and I do not have cable nor satellite TV. What we see on TV, comes to us through the internet. We watch some things on Hulu and Amazon Prime. That means we have to endure their commercials, which we generally deplore. The worst ones are for tv series they are producing and selling. Generally, they are dark, even Satanic. We marvel that there is an audience for this awful stuff. We see it from our perspective as Christians. It is easy for us to forget that those who do not know Jesus are blind to spiritual truth, they live in darkness and in the power of Satan.

I realize as I write this there are people in the church who will find these words harsh, judgmental, unkind, and even prejudiced or bigoted. However, that does not change the reality of the condition of a soul apart from Jesus. Blind, dark, Satanic. "And such were some of you." However, through the power of the glorious good news of the Gospel of Jesus, they "may receive forgiveness of sins and a place among those who are sanctified by faith in Jesus."

Transactional and Transformational

Please note the two critical aspects of this salvation. One is transactional: the forgiveness of sins. It is as though every sin you ever committed was written on a white board, then they are removed forever through the blood of Jesus. The other aspect of salvation is sanctification. This is transformational. Not only are our sins forgiven, we are made holy and set aside for God's purposes.

Many in the church claim the forgiveness of sins, but ignore the whole notion of holy living. There are even those who will describe what the Bible calls an "abomination" as holy living.

Paul was sent to those who were spiritually blind, who lived in darkness, who lived in the power of Satan to preach Jesus to them so they could be forgiven and sanctified. Paul was faithful to that heavenly vision.

Are you? Am I? Folks are still, blind, in darkness, living in the power of Satan. Who will tell them of the forgiveness of sins and the sanctified, holy life? Will you? Will I?

Thoughts of the day

Prayer list.

1.
2.
3.
4.
5.
6.
7.
8.

Through the Storm

Read Acts 27

Last night an angel of the God to whom I belong and whom I serve stood beside me and said,'Do not be afraid, Paul. You must stand trial before Caesar; and God has graciously given you the lives of all who sail with you.'

Acts 27:23,24.

This whole chapter is about Paul being transported across the Mediterranean Sea to Rome to face trial before Caesar. The heart of the chapter tells the story of the terrible storm they endured including the loss of everything on the ship and even the ship itself.

All the soldiers and sailors were terrified of the horrible storm that buffeted them for several days. However, in the dark of night the Lord sent his messenger to Paul to assure him that he would survive the storm, as would all who sailed with him. Paul told his fellow travelers what the Lord's messenger had said. Sure enough, they were all spared even though everything of earthly value was lost.

Why does Luke record this long story in such detail? Couldn't he have used this space to give us greater insight into the ministry of Paul or Paul's theology and teaching?

One can only guess, but it can be an educated guess. Luke, the physician, had often cared for people who were going through the worst storms of life. They were sick, injured, or dying. They may have just lost a child or parent or a spouse in a most cruel, even violent way. My best guess is Luke, in the inspiration of the Holy Spirit, told of this very traumatic event in the life of Paul, and yes even his own life as a passenger with Paul, to give hope and comfort to his readers. When life becomes a deadly storm., even if we lose everything of material value, the Lord promises to be with us through the storm.

That is enough.

Thoughts of the day

Prayer list.

1.
2.
3.
4.
5.
6.
7.
8.

The Acts Will Continue...

Read Acts 28

"For two whole years Paul stayed there in his own rented house and welcomed all who came to see him. He proclaimed the kingdom of God and taught about the Lord Jesus Christ—with all boldness and without hindrance!"

Acts 28:30,31

This chapter describes the rest of the journey to Rome including miracles, signs, and wonders Paul performed resulting in more people coming to saving faith in Jesus. The story is fascinating and reminds us of what Luke had reported The Resurrected Jesus said to his disciples in Acts 1:8, "But you will receive power when the Holy Spirit comes on you; and you will be my witnesses in Jerusalem, and in all Judea and Samaria, and to the ends of the earth."

Paul, even as a prisoner, ministered in the power of the Holy Spirit and took the Gospel to the center of power in the Western world: Rome.

"He proclaimed the kingdom of God and taught about the Lord Jesus Christ—with all boldness and without hindrance!"

The End.
Or is it?

Thoughts of the day

Prayer list.

1.
2.
3.
4.
5.
6.
7.
8.

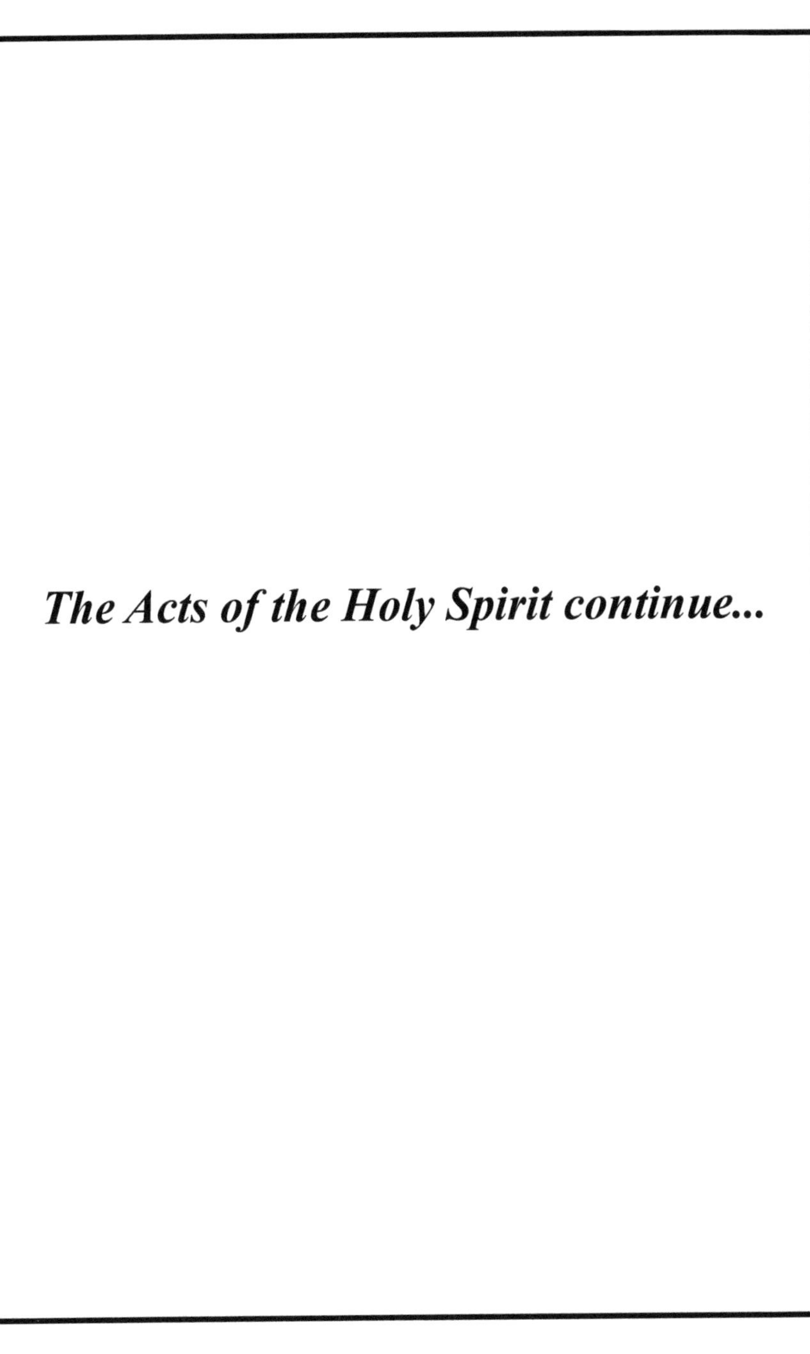

The Acts of the Holy Spirit continue...

www.ingramcontent.com/pod-product-compliance
Ingram Content Group UK Ltd.
Pitfield, Milton Keynes, MK11 3LW, UK
UKHW020418250726
13967UKWH00007B/2707

9 781435 766495